Winning
at
Interview

Winning at Interview

A NEW WAY TO SUCCEED

Alan Jones

RANDOM HOUSE

BUSINESS BOOKS

3 5 7 9 10 8 6 4

Alan Jones has asserted his rights under the Copyright, Designs and
Patents Act, 1988 to be identified as the author of this work

First published in 2000 by Random House Business Books,
Random House, 20 Vauxhall Bridge Road, London SW1V 2SA

Random House Australia (Pty) Limited
20 Alfred Street, Milsons Point, Sydney
New South Wales 2061, Australia

Random House New Zealand Limited
18 Poland Road, Glenfield,
Auckland 10, New Zealand

Random House (Pty) Limited
Endulini, 5A Jubilee Road, Parktown 2193, South Africa

The Random House Group Limited Reg. No. 954009

Papers used by Random House are natural, recyclable products made
from wood grown in sustainable forests. The manufacturing processes
conform to the environmental regulations of the country of origin

ISBN 0 7126 7019 X

Companies, institutions and other organizations wishing to make
bulk purchases of any business books published by Random House
should contact their local bookstore or Random House direct:

Special Sales Director
Random House, 20 Vauxhall Bridge Road, London SW1V 2SA
Te: 020 7840 8470   Fax: 020 7828 6681
businessbooks@randomhouse.co.uk

www.randomhouse.co.uk
businessbooks@randomhouse.co.uk

Typeset by SX Composing DTP, Rayleigh, Essex
Printed and Bound in Great Britain by Bookmarque Ltd, Croydon, Surrey

Contents

Foreword

Job hunting is a serious business, but if it were a game it might be described as follows:

This is a game for any number of players. The game is divided into two halves: the first half is called Application, the second half is called Interview. All players will begin the first half but not all will be playing in the second half. The object of the game is to achieve the job offer and there can only be one winner. In the first half of the game, each player must overcome certain hazards designed to prevent him or her from qualifying for the second half. Typical application hazards are too old, lacks experience, job hopper and not qualified. Players who successfully negotiate these hazards are declared winners and will go on to play Interview. Further hazards are encountered at Interview, including no confidence, talks too much, shifty, untidy etc. At the conclusion of the game the player who has overcome all of the hazards is declared the winner and receives the job offer. All remaining players, who had previously been winners are now losers.

Now, what makes this game particularly interesting is that few players can play both halves of the game equally well. One player may be a star turn when playing Application but a consummate duffer at Interview. Conversely, another player might play an excellent game of Interview but won't get the chance to prove it until the Application hazards can be overcome. But what is it that separates the winners from the losers? The eventual winner of the game is not necessarily the best person for the job. Indeed, the best person for the job is frequently eliminated in the first half. No, the winner of the game will always be *the player who has played the game the best . . .* Knowing how to play the game is the secret of success.

These words first appeared in the Introduction to *How to Write a Winning CV* (Random House Business Books). Many readers have told me how much it has helped them to improve their game in the first half but asked how they might discover the rules of 'Interview'. *Winning at Interview* fills that need.

Introduction

What *is* a job interview? Typically, and unfortunately, it is a sales meeting between two parties, one with little concept of what they are selling and the other with only a vague understanding of what they need to buy. Small wonder, then, that these exercises in communication invariably end in tears – largely through the inability of both parties to listen, understand and evaluate.

A person of my acquaintance was interviewed for an administrative position. Apparently all was well until he was faced with the question 'What is your greatest weakness?' He replied, in effect, 'I am not very good at administration.' Naturally enough, this show stopper precluded him from being invited back. Now this was a bit of a puzzle as I knew him to be an excellent administrator, so why did he say otherwise? 'Well, there were three of them sitting there and I felt a bit outgunned. I hadn't prepared for the question, the silence was deafening, my brain seized up and I just said the first stupid thing that came into my head.' Through lack of preparation he admitted to a weakness he didn't have. He gave up on the question, lost the plot and the job offer. Does it serve him right for telling a lie?

I know one interviewer who begins every interview by saying 'Tell me about yourself' and reaches for the smelling salts when she gets the response, as she invariably does, 'What would you like to know?' Although this is not the best way to start an interview, I can understand her anguish. Imagine that you have a product to sell. After much effort on your part the potential buyer agrees to meet you and says, 'I'm extremely busy and don't have much time – so tell me about your product.' Are you *really* going to say, 'What would you like to know?' Many people do, or they mumble a few incoherent words and quickly run out of ideas or, even worse, bore the buyer rigid with an unending diatribe of irrelevant and damaging information, largely based upon how old the damn product is.

Why do we do ourselves such a disservice at interviews? *Because we've only turned up to get a job.* Our minds are solely focused on what for us is the big problem: we don't have a job and boy do we need one – bad. The greater our need the worse our performance. In my experience there are fundamentally two types of interviewee. The majority are 'job beggars' who, by virtue of what they say and how they say it, quickly give the impression that the only reason they have come to the interview is because they need a job. The minority – and these are the ones who get hired – give the impression that they are pleased to be at the interview and would have turned up even if they still had a job. The term 'job beggar' may seem unsympathetic and pejorative but I do not intend it to be – it is simply the way we are. How do we become 'job beggars'? When we 'lose a job' we make the mistake of taking ownership of the problem and this expresses itself in the signals we send: 'Having recently been made redundant, I am writing to ask if you have any vacancies . . .' can be interpreted as 'I've got a problem and am hoping you can solve it by giving me a job'. Could we really blame the employer for thinking 'I'm not in business to solve your problems. I'm in business to make a profit. If you had told me how you can help me achieve that, I might have been pleased to meet you, but as it is, the best I can do is put your letter on this thick rejection file over here.'

Problems arise at interviews, then, because each party is working to a different agenda. The employer is seeking to find someone to fill a particular role, which is not always clearly defined, while the prospective employee is looking to find a job. This dichotomy, where each party is dancing to a different tune, has proved to be the rock on which many an interview has foundered.

To find a way forward we must take a radically new view and redefine our understanding of a lot of things, not least the nature of the employer/employee relationship. To achieve this we must not only ask 'what is an interview?' but 'what is a *job*?' A *job* is no more than *a means of fulfilling a need profitably*, and the relationship between employer and employee is no more than a *buyer/seller* relationship. There was a time when we liked to believe that it was a bit more cosy than that, but that was in the days when we thought organisations existed solely for the purpose of employing people. That no one *wants* to hire us is initially somewhat worrying, but it's nothing personal – they don't want to hire anyone else either.

The changing world of work in the twentieth century spawned a new language to describe the ways in which labour was bought and sold. Words such as 'job', 'employer', 'employee', 'retirement', 'salary' and yes, 'interview' all became current coinage, and they were not much used before then. They *belong* to the twentieth century and that is where we must leave them as they won't serve us well in the twenty-first. We are now moving from a *job*-based employment culture to a *work*-based self-employed society. To ease this transition our language must change accordingly. The baggage that went along with the job-begging culture must be jettisoned if we are to adapt to this new world of work. This book will reflect that. The 'job' is something we will leave behind – it's no longer a neat way to parcel up work. While we are at it, let's be bold and consign the word 'interview' to the historical garbage bin. I for one won't miss it – it was always too close to 'inquisition' and perhaps that's why it made us nervous. You may find yourself attending 'interviews' for 'jobs' in the old-fashioned sense for some time yet, but in this book we will understand them for what they are – sales meeting where you, the seller, are seeking to convince the buyer to hire your services. The buyer is the one with the problem – you are the solution. *Winning at Interview* will demonstrate why, if you focus on the buyer's need and show how you can fulfil it, you'll get hired.

ONE Preparation Prevents Poor Performance

The battle is largely won or lost before you even show up. It's really a matter of preparation and damage control. Imagine that in going to the meeting you are a ship sailing into a war zone. You would have to be quite fortunate to sail away from that war zone without having had a few holes blown in your rigging. But if you do your damage control preparation before entering you are equally unlikely to be sunk by the first salvo.

> Further to your application for this position, we have pleasure in inviting you to an interview at the above address at 2 p.m. on Friday, 13 May. When you arrive, please ask for Mr John Smith.

Any elation you may feel at having clinched the meeting should be tempered by a degree of curiosity. Your competitors are likely to do no more than make a note in the diary and carry on snoozing. If you snooze you lose. Two questions need to be asked:

1   What are they telling me?
2   What are they *not* telling me?

You have a place, a date, a starting time and a name. The bare minimum information you need simply to turn up. What pieces in the jigsaw are missing?

1   Who is this mysterious Mr Smith? You might assume that he is the person they have designated to conduct the meeting. Assume nothing. Stories are legion of the unprepared turning up, being greeted by a 'Mr Smith' whose only function is to lead them, as lambs to the slaughter, to an office in which resides a panel of interlocutors. Not being psyched up for a panel, and not knowing who these individuals are, can seriously disturb one's mental equilibrium before getting one's coat off. Surprises like this are both unnecessary and avoidable.

2. You will of course always be given a starting time but rarely any indication of the scheduled duration – unless you request it. Never assume that 'it will take as long as it takes' or be content with some vague notion that it should take 'an hour or so'. The chances are high that you will be seen by someone inexperienced, unprepared and inclined to waste the first twenty minutes telling you his life story. He may then realise that time is running out, make heroic efforts to ask you some meaningful questions about your suitability for the role but then, ten minutes later, start winding it up by saying, 'Right, I've got someone else to see now. Thank you for coming – I've enjoyed talking to you [which is all he's done], we'll be in touch.' So that was a meeting which was only ever designed to last thirty minutes, twenty of which were wasted, and you leave without having sold a thing. If you clarify this *before* the

meeting and establish that only thirty minutes have been allocated then at least you will be psychologically prepared. Is there anything you can do about it? You can, on first meeting the other party, issue a gentle reminder: 'Am I right in thinking that we have just half an hour?' This is a polite enough way of saying, 'Get your skates on because I can't sell much in thirty minutes if you don't allow me to, so don't tell me your life story.'

Telephoning beforehand and asking 'How much time has been allocated for the meeting?' often elicits, quite voluntarily, further information about your competition and the pecking order. This is 'nice to know' rather than 'need to know' information but the more pieces of the jigsaw you hold the better.

Knowing the anticipated timing has two other benefits: it will dictate your *pace* during the meeting and it will help you to predict when the 'End Game' (page 59) might kick in.

> *You are going to the meeting to make a sale – you need to know how long you've got to make it.*

3   Is there any written information about their problem – sometimes called a 'Job Description'? These purport to describe the role accurately but rarely do so. Nevertheless, if there is one and you can encourage the buyer to send it to you prior to the meeting then you have more information than your competitors, which must be an advantage.

4   What do you know about the buyer's organisation? They generally expect you to be able to tell them something about their business – it shows initiative and courtesy. Yet this research doesn't have to be a cloak-and-dagger exercise. Using directories and websites is fine, but why not get them to send you something? 'I'd naturally like to come as prepared as possible – could you send me some information prior to the

meeting?' It matters not whether they say yes or no, in just asking the question you are already opening up a dialogue and selling yourself. Incidentally, your buyer may still be using that twentieth-century word 'interview' but it doesn't mean that *you* have to. In any dialogue or correspondence with the buyer you refer to a 'meeting' – you will feel better and it more accurately makes the point that it is a two-way process.

TWO

So – Communicate!

Selling yourself is no more than an exercise in communication and on the whole it is something that we tend not to be very good at. We don't communicate when we should and we communicate sometimes when it would be more prudent not to do so. Once a line of communication has been opened up the general rule, and one to which it is worth subscribing, is to keep it open. It is useful to see this in terms of a tennis match and throughout the process of self-marketing one should ask, 'Whose got the ball?' Having received the ball in the form of an invitation to a meeting, it would be courteous and businesslike to return it by communicating that one would be pleased to attend. The snoozers' thought processes rarely get this far so this is an opportunity for you to score a few points and 'make a friend at Court'. This can be achieved by a simple telephone call. Now going about this in the wrong way can easily result in your making an enemy rather than a friend. Simply ringing up and launching into your agenda is a sure-fire way of doing it. Always give the other party the option of putting the phone down, e.g.: 'I am ringing to confirm that I will be pleased to attend at 2 p.m. on 13 May – there are a few things that I need to clarify but if it's not convenient I can ring back later.' If the other party gives the green light, then fine – ask questions about anything you feel needs clarifying. It is useful to have your 'need to know' questions in some semblance of order as you may feel it inappropriate to ask all of them. This is a fine call and only you can judge the right moment to end the conversation. If you sense that you are really hitting it off with the other person you can sometimes get down to the small talk. 'I guess you had a lot of applications for the position?' can get them to reveal how many applied and how many of those they are seeing. Again, you don't need this information but it is nice to know what you are up against. The crucial questions are those regarding whom you will be seeing and the timing of the meeting – anything else is a bonus.

Having knocked the communication ball over the net, you would not expect any further communication before the meeting (unless you got them to agree to send you a job description and/or company information). However, don't relax yet. Consider knocking another ball over the net, i.e. communicate *in writing* that you will be pleased to attend.

The good thing about a telephone call is that it can, and often should, be followed up by a letter – an altogether more tangible communication:

Further to your letter dated 25 April and our subsequent conversation/my subsequent discussion with your secretary, I am writing to confirm that I will indeed be pleased to meet both yourself and Mrs Brown at 2 p.m. on 13 May.

Thank you for agreeing to send me a copy of the Job Description and an Annual Report in the interim period, which I look forward to receiving.

This acts as a reminder for them to send it and that you had the initiative to ask for it. In these days of instant electronic communication, letter writing has gone out of fashion but do not completely eschew the letter as a means of communication when selling yourself – it retains the benefits of being more personal, intimate and more classy. Speed is not everything, so don't sacrifice quality for it.

By now you may be forgiven for thinking, 'This is tiresome – do I really have to do all this?' The short answer is 'No, of course you don't' but that is the point – successful self-marketing is about taking the time and trouble to do those things that will make you stand out from the competition. You are setting up the meeting by, at this early stage, presenting the buyer with a body of evidence to suggest that you, and no other, are worth hiring. Looking at it another way, if you choose to be a snoozer you might, just might, be competing with someone who has bothered to do these things while you are not even on the starting blocks. It will always be your call.

THREE Your Five Point Plan

Failing to prepare really is preparing to fail but there is more to it than simply trying to anticipate the issues that might arise at the meeting and practising your sales pitch. Most sellers are defeated before the meeting because they are not psychologically in tune with the situation – the mind set is out of synch, in much the same way that a boxer can be 'psyched out' before going into the ring, despite having put in the physical training.

To ensure that your mental attitude is positive you can have your own five-point plan based on the following.

1   *Beware of your objective and stay true to it.* Your primary objective in attending the meeting is to get the buyer to make you an offer, which you do not have until it is in writing. Until you have that written offer you have no decision to make. If I could put the previous sentence in neon lights I would do so, for in losing sight of the objective you can lose everything. Sellers have an alarming habit of making a pre-emptive decision, e.g. during the meeting, that they don't want to solve the buyer's problem. This is a common mistake and it is all too easy to understand why it happens. The meeting is no more than a fact-finding tour for both parties. You will not have all

the facts upon which to base a sound judgement until you receive the written offer. Even then there are often issues that require further clarification.

Problems arise when buyers divulge facts about their problem, the organisation, their perceived solution and not least the price, which serve to make you feel less enamoured about the whole idea. If you are not focused your attitude and demeanour will reflect this through visible lack of enthusiasm and a diminishing performance. This can be infectious. If the buyer catches it you will reach a mutual decision that there is little point in taking it to the next stage. That's a round one knockout to the buyer. Never assume that buyers know what they are looking for, particularly at the first meeting when very little may be defined, although they might be desperate to give the impression that they understand the extent of their problem. I have worked with many sellers who, having received an excellent offer, are grateful that they stayed true to their objective – issues that appeared insurmountable during the stress and strain of the meeting had either paled into insignificance or disappeared altogether by the time the offer was made. The turbulent waters of these meetings can throw up a lot of garbage. Navigate your way through, put clear water between yourself and the buyer, and then make an informed decision in the calmer waters of your own territory.

2   *Beware the well-meaning advice to 'be yourself'.* This is the worst advice anyone can give you before the meeting and it isn't worth a row of beans. This doesn't mean that you have to try to be someone else, nor that you should try to change your innate character and personality. To a greater or lesser degree we all role-play in what we do. We wear different 'hats' for different occasions. Our boxer might be a nice, gentle person outside the ring but his trainer would be ill advised to say, 'It's fight night tonight but just go in that ring and be yourself.' Now many a seller has turned up to a sales meeting with their 'business hat' on their head, but has left that meeting with

their 'social hat' perched at a cocky angle, having had a great chat with the buyer – but without having sold a damn thing. A professional buyer will always try to deformalise the meeting and relax the seller. Why is it that when these meetings are held in a social setting, e.g. over lunch, they are notoriously difficult to handle? Because in those situations the informality of the occasion seduces us into being our 'social selves' and this is reflected in what we say and how we say it. When people advise you to 'be yourself' they are, unwittingly, giving you permission to do no preparation. They are saying 'WYSIWYG (what you see is what you get)', 'It's in the lap of the Gods', 'They either like you or they don't'. This really isn't good enough. Whether you like it or not, you are going into a sales meeting and you say whatever it takes to achieve your objective. Once the offer is achieved you can then decide if you can (and want) to deliver. If you feel that you can't 'walk the talk', then turn it down – you'll be doing yourself and the buyer a favour.

3   *At the first meeting all sellers are equal.* If your sales literature (CV and covering letter) has done its job and encouraged the buyer to want to meet you, then at the very least that buyer is saying, 'Based on what I've read, I believe that you could *possibly* be the solution to my problem.' Now you may be competing with someone who has, on paper, a higher credibility rating, in which case the buyer is saying, 'Based on what I've read I believe that you could *probably* be the solution to my problem.' So on paper not all sellers are equal – there is a pecking order. At the meeting this can be turned on its head within the first thirty seconds. The heart of many a buyer has sunk on meeting a 'probable' who on paper appeared to be a candidate for canonisation but who is ill prepared, poorly turned out and has a personality problem. Don't go into these meetings feeling vulnerable about lack of qualifications or experience – to a degree those 'weaknesses' have already been overcome. If you can sell the positives and defend the

negatives you can turn yourself from a 'possible' into a 'probable'. It is a truism that those who achieve the offer are not always the best equipped for the task – but they are always the ones who have sold themselves best.

4   *Always retain your self-respect.* It is crucial that you not only 'walk tall' into these sales meetings but that you walk tall coming away from them. Remember that you always have the power of veto, i.e. you can terminate the meeting at any stage. Very rarely, if ever, will you have to exercise that power, but if the buyer is treating you as a 'job beggar' then exercise it you must. No one ever forgets a bad experience and too many sellers have a horror story to tell about a meeting where the buyer treated them with disrespect and they regret not having walked away with their self-esteem intact. You neither want nor need to carry that emotional baggage around with you for the rest of your life.

There is the story, perhaps apocryphal, of the seller who was being treated particularly discourteously by a panel of buyers. He decided to exercise his veto saying, 'I feel that you are wasting my time, good day to you.' Whereupon one of the buyers jumped to his feet saying, 'But wait – you are just the person we are looking for!' The seller replied, 'Perhaps, but I'm not looking for you' and carried on walking. You should consider whether you would be happy working with an organisation that uses heavy-handed tactics. Losing your self-respect can lower your confidence level at subsequent meetings with other organisations. This is not to suggest that you should terminate a meeting just because it gets tough – you want to stick around for those to test your technique and you need as much practice as you can get. If, on going into the meeting, your mindset is telling you 'I hope they'll want to hire me' then you are a dead duck. It should be saying, 'It's your lucky day because I'm now giving you an opportunity to hire me. Based on my understanding of your problem, I'm the solution so don't give me a hard time. Ask me the right questions and I will endeavour to provide the right answers. Oh, and by the way, if you make me an offer don't assume that I'm going to bite your hand off – I may subsequently decide that I don't want to solve your problem.' Never forget who has the problem – job beggars think they have it.

5   *You should feel 'nervous' before the meeting.* Most sellers are, but for all the wrong reasons. Professional actors expect to feel nervous before a performance. This is because they have attended all the rehearsals. They know their lines inside out and when the curtain goes up they want all that hard work and preparation to be reflected in their performance. Amateurs may have missed a few rehearsals, be shaky on their lines, know it and be nervous because when the curtain goes up they are hoping that it won't show. It will. So it's not 'nerves' per se that are the problem. If you feel nervous before the meeting, ask yourself why. Let your competitors be too busy being nervous to think about winning.

FOUR Dead Zone One

Your arrival at the venue for the meeting, ideally fifteen minutes before the appointed hour, can signal the beginning of unforeseeable events. This period of time – after your arrival but before the meeting gets under way – is of unpredictable length and indeterminate nature. We will call it 'Dead Zone One'. You have done your homework and points four and five of your Five-Point Plan are of particular importance in the Dead Zone. You should now be giving a good impression to everyone you meet – receptionists and security staff can exercise much influence on the decision makers. Display civility and not servility.

Although judgements are being made of you by others as soon as you enter the Dead Zone the two-way process begins here, so how do you feel about them? There are a number of things for which you should be on the lookout:

1 Are they organised? Did they know you were coming? Do they appear to be pleased to see you or do they give the impression that they don't much care whether you turned up or not?

2 Do they keep you waiting an inordinate length of time without explanation or apology? These meetings do have a notorious

reputation for over-running. This is where points one and four of your Five-Point Plan may come into conflict – you may be making negative judgements about their offhand and casual treatment of you, and this may cause you to lose sight of your objective. But if this is how they are treating you now, then how will they treat you once you join them? Is it time to exercise your veto?

3   What environment do they provide for their people? Don't be fooled by the 'corporate plumage'. The impressive display you might see in the more public areas is not necessarily duplicated elsewhere. This highlights the importance of your making a point of asking to see where you might be working (page 66).

4   Is there any business going on? Do they look successful? Not always possible to get an accurate assessment of this – some successful organisations exude an air of quiet efficiency rather than scenes of frenetic activity. But if no phones are ringing and you see people idly chatting around the photocopier then take note. You don't want to join a sinking ship.

5   Has any literature or other material been deliberately left lying around for you to notice? This is no time for snoozing. Be alert and observant.

6   What is their style? Look at the people you see coming and going. Do *they* look happy to be working there? Listen to conversations. If you see someone who is clearly a senior executive speaking with a junior member of staff, how is the conversation conducted, in a friendly or autocratic manner?

It is possible that your concentration on the above matters will serve to make you quite unaware of the buyer standing patiently over you, trying to get your attention. They appear from nowhere. You are about to leave Dead Zone One and it's now showtime.

FIVE So – Why Should I Hire You?

We would like to believe that these meetings are more than just question and answer sessions, but the basic truth is that the buyer asks questions, you respond and judgements are made on those responses. It is impossible to predict every question that might arise, although there are some old chestnuts that appear time and again. Success lies in your ability to anticipate the questions, analyse and interpret them as accurately as possible, and prepare your responses. Where do you start? Because there are so many potential questions this might at first sight appear difficult but if we apply a little logic it becomes less daunting.

Fundamentally there are only two questions the buyer can ask!

1 Why should I hire you?
2 Why shouldn't I hire you?

Just about any question you might care to think of will fall into one of the above categories. Your success depends upon your ability to distinguish the good questions from the dangerous ones. Question 1 above is the only question you have turned up to answer. Go unprepared and you will leave the meeting having wasted more time on question 2, and consequently given the buyer more reasons why you shouldn't be hired.

The theory will now be tested. There follows a selection of typical questions, each of which is denoted by the symbol ✓ or ✗. Questions denoted ✓ are the good 'Why should I hire you?' questions. These are the ones that are not inherently dangerous. You *want* these questions and you *love* them because they give you an opportunity to sell yourself. The others, denoted ✗, are potentially dangerous and are inviting you to shoot yourself in the foot. They require deft handling and evasive action as any one of them can blow you clean out of the water.

How was your journey? ✓

Even this seemingly innocuous ice-breaker can be turned by the unguarded into a ✗ question. A bore is someone who, when you ask them how they are, actually tells you. This question falls into the same category. There is no overt hidden agenda but even if your journey to the meeting was a nightmare, resist the temptation to say so. They will conclude that if you are going to have that problem at the beginning and end of every day they may as well not hire you. You might consider selling your planning skills by saying, 'Fine – I took the precaution of checking it out beforehand.' Don't. Buyers might be unprofessional but they are rarely that dumb. This question can make an early appearance during 'Dead Zone One'.

Tell me about yourself ✗

This is not going to crop up halfway through the meeting but is most likely to hit you as soon as you have walked through the door and sat down. This is not generally recognised as being a particularly good way to begin one of these meetings but as most buyers are ill prepared this might account for its frequency. It is, however, a most excellent question to get, but only if you are prepared for it. Because it will come at the beginning it has a particular importance in that it *sets the standard* for the rest of the meeting. Respond well and you have laid a solid foundation upon which to build. It also sets the standard for your competitors as the chances are high that they too will be faced with it.

If you fail to prepare for this, almost certainly one of three things will happen.

1 You may be tempted to ask the buyer to clarify the question. Don't. There is no advantage in your doing so. Never assume that buyers know why they are asking this or indeed any other question. It is more likely that the buyer is really saying, 'I'm unprepared for this meeting. I have no structure or agenda so you start and we'll see where the conversation takes us.' If you say 'what do you want to know?' they will be forced to pluck something out of the air, which might not be in your interests.

2 You will make heroic efforts to deal with it but through the lack of a script it will all wither on the vine after about thirty seconds. You will have started badly, wasted what is a great question to get and feel embarrassed about it. Your body language will all too visibly convey that you have run out of ideas and the buyer will have to come to the rescue in an effort to breathe some new life into the meeting.

3 It may be your nervous reaction to start talking and not know when to stop. At the end of twenty minutes you will have presented the buyer with a long, rambling discourse of irrelevant, disjointed and damaging information, and have no idea what supplementary questions might follow. You can do a lot of damage in twenty minutes. Sellers have an alarming habit of bringing their emotional baggage to these meetings

and dumping it in the buyer's lap at the first opportunity. 'Tell me about yourself' provides the perfect opportunity because it is such an open question. It is quite astonishing how many people begin their response by telling the buyer how old they are. Many people do feel vulnerable about their age but why put it on the table? Buyers are more likely to have a problem with it once sellers indicate that *they* see it as an issue.

Before the meeting always assume that you will get this question. You *want* it because it is the archetypal 'Why should I hire you?' question. It's a blank cheque, so fill it in. Look carefully at your understanding of their need. Be objective and ask yourself, 'Well – why *should* they hire me? What can I bring to their party?' It's worth remembering that they must, at the very least, believe that you could possibly be the right person, otherwise they wouldn't be wasting their time. What has attracted them? Identify these things, make a list and build a script around them. Write it all out, refine it, read it aloud, time it. Two minutes is about right – you can sell a lot of good things in two minutes provided you are focused.

Once you have your script, look at it again and take it a stage further. Ask yourself, 'If I say these things, what supplementary questions might they come up with?' It doesn't require a great deal of creativity and imagination to then ask yourself, 'Well, what supplementary questions would I *like* them to come up with?' With sound preparation you can decide the direction in which you want the meeting to go. You can actually make the buyer ask you the question you would rather get, not the one that will arise as the result of an off-the-cuff remark from you. Received wisdom has it that buyers should be in control of the meeting. It is, after all, taking place on their territory and at their behest. To an extent this is correct but prepared sellers can exert a high degree of influence and subtlety, which will allow them to direct the course of the discussion, but not in such a way that they wrest control from the buyer. For example, anything to do with 'problems' is meat and drink to the buyer. If you deliberately allude to a 'problem' in your script but choose not to elaborate on it buyers will fall upon such a delicacy like a dog with a bone because it tempts them to ask supplementary ✗ questions such as: '*What problem and how did you solve it?*' Now if you had referred to this problem without thinking then it would remain a ✗ question and you would be fighting a rearguard action. But if you deliberately provoked the supplementary to provide a further opportunity to sell, then it is in reality a ✓ question. One great virtue of preparing a script is that you will know where the full stop is at least meant to be.

What do you know about us? ✓

What you know is less important than being able to display that you have taken the trouble to find out something about the organisation. It sells initiative and courtesy. It is particularly impressive if you can tell them something that *they* don't know, but this is more a matter of luck than judgement. If the organisation has a 'presence in the high street', i.e. if they have retail outlets or branches that you could visit as a customer prior to the meeting, then it is essential that you do so, otherwise huge embarrassment can result: '*When you were last in one of our branches, did you notice anything that particularly impressed you?*' ✓ and '*Did you notice anything that you feel we could improve upon?*' ✗. If you have to admit that you haven't even been into one of their branches then although the buyer will continue with the meeting you have been mentally consigned to an early bath. With ✗ do not be too critical. You may be talking to the person whose remit it is, or if there are two or more buyers at the meeting one of them may be responsible for that part of the business about which you are complaining – you can make an enemy without knowing it. It is generally expected that buyers will have done their homework and failure to do so can turn a 'probable' into a 'possible' (see page 10) or, even worse, if the buyer sees it as a crucial issue. Don't expect *all* buyers to ask this question (see page 63).

Why does this role interest you? ✓

It can interest you for many valid reasons and you would normally
be quite safe putting any of them on the table. Avoid clichés like
the plague. There is certainly nothing wrong with a 'challenge' yet
voice it and you will most likely see the buyer's eyes glaze over – it
is a sign that you are bereft of any real ideas. Why might they
want it to interest you? Presumably because of what you think you
can *bring* to it in terms of skills, experience and perhaps personal
qualities – try to place the emphasis on these things and not so
much on what you can get from it, e.g. 'challenge', 'career
progression'. This is an opportunity for you to 'make the match'
and impress on them that you are the solution to their problem.

Why are you leaving/did you leave your present/previous position? ✗

Hidden agenda: 'Are you leaving/did you leave for any reasons
that might make me *not* want to hire you?' The buyer may not
realise that this is the hidden agenda but the wrong response from
you will reveal it. In pure recruitment terms there is only one valid
reason for leaving one organisation and joining another: to
broaden one's experience. In reality we all understand that there
are various reasons why we move – some more acceptable than
others. Many of us find ourselves in the market for work as a
result of change, e.g. 're-engineering', 'downsizing', and no
sensible buyers would have a problem with it. However, sellers do
themselves a huge disservice by the way in which they express it.
The cardinal sin is simply to say, 'I've been made redundant'. Look
at it closely and you will see that there is something pathetic
about it. It is the seller as victim. Such an answer is both negative
and misleading. It sends the following signals:

- The seller and no one else has been selected for redundancy.
  This is rarely the case.

- The seller is a 'job beggar' (see page x).
- There is more to 'uncover' about this redundancy. 'I've been made redundant' will almost certainly lead to a litany of supplementary questions, many of which are ✗ but at best are wasting time. For 'Human Resource' specialists redundancy is the sticky part of their role and they will, if given the opportunity, show a keen interest in it, e.g. *That must have been disappointing – how do you feel about it?* ✗ and *How well do you think your company handled it?* ✗. As there is no mileage whatsoever in these supplementary questions it is far better to close it off in such a way that the buyer will be reassured, lose interest in pursuing it and move on to the more ✓ questions.

Devise a response that has three parts to it, a beginning, a middle and an end:

Part 1   Give the buyers a time frame within which they can mentally operate: '*Over the past year.*' This lets them know from the outset that you did not have to leave as the result of some overnight 'knee-jerk' decision by the company. Now use the word 'change' and/or 'restructuring': '*There has been a lot of change through restructuring.*' This is a concept with which they are familiar and their interest is already waning. Don't give your opinion on it – opinions can be dangerous, so don't let the word 'unfortunately' creep in.

Part 2   Tell them what the result of that change has been in terms of the number of jobs (not 'people') that have been affected: '*During this period thirty jobs have become surplus to requirements and mine is one of them.*' This gives them the big picture and the accurate one. Note that *jobs* are made redundant, not *people*. Taking ownership of the redundancy word is to be discouraged – it belongs to the buyers not the sellers.

Part 3   Now end on a high note. A note of optimism, enthusiasm and of the future rather than the past: '*Although I've really enjoyed my previous role I'm now seeing this as an opportunity to use my skills in an organisation like yours.*' This tells them that you feel just fine about the whole débâcle, thus preventing them from asking you. Now encourage them to ask a 'Why should I hire you?' question: '*Because I believe I have a lot to offer.*' The supplementary question *What have you got to offer?* ✓ is virtually irresistible and providing you are prepared then this will be a road along which you are more than happy to travel. On the whole, buyers are not used to meeting sellers who have come prepared to say what they have to offer, so there is a strong intrigue factor here. Brevity is important with ✗ questions. The more time you spend on them the more danger you are in of getting bogged down. It should take no more than ten to fifteen seconds to deal with this question.

Why did you stay with them for so long? ✗

This is an implied criticism with the hidden agenda that you suffer from inertia and have no ambition to progress. Time was when staying with the same organisation for the whole of one's working life 'womb to tomb' was very much the norm. It showed commendable qualities such as commitment and loyalty. For some it was the perfect vehicle for a rewarding career. For many more it provided no more than a welcome security blanket. Now that employers have taken their blankets back, people are hung out to dry in the chill wind of an ever changing marketplace populated by 'buyers' and 'sellers'. That's progress. Fortunately, 'progress' is the key to this question. If there is evidence to show that you didn't stand still then you must put it on the table and defend yourself against this unfair accusation: '*Although I was with them for twenty years you will see from my CV that I wasn't getting the same experience twenty times over.*' We need not necessarily be talking about promotion here. A succession of different roles at the same level is enough and is in its own way progression: '*I always felt that I was making a positive contribution to the organisation.*' You could perhaps end your response by pointing out that you believed that you were always giving 'added value' to your role. This begs the supplementaries *What particular value do you feel you added to that role?* ✓ and *What added value can you bring to this role?* ✓.

'Endings' are really quite important. Invariably the supplementary questions will arise from the last thing the buyer heard you say. Taking care over what you are going to say and *how* you are going to say it can pay real dividends.

You seem to have done a lot of job hopping – why? ✗

Hidden agendas: you haven't found your niche in life; you lack commitment; you can't hold down a role for any reasonable length of time; you don't get on with people; you are unreliable. They almost certainly won't want to hire you if any one of these is true. It is not necessary for you to explain, and least of all apologise for, each change you have made. If the changes you made allowed you to broaden your experience then say so: '*Ideally I would prefer to stay with the same organisation, but so far I have found that to broaden my experience I have had to move outside the company to achieve it. For example . . .*' Now give an example of a good career move, explain the rationale behind it and leave it at that. In these times of constant and unremitting change, buyers do not really expect anyone to stay with them for the whole of their working lives and yet they invariably expect sellers to send 'commitment' signals that suggest that they might do just that.

What is your greatest strength? ✓

This is a gift, so grab it with both hands. Interpret the question as: 'Give me one reason why I should hire you?' It is quite astonishing how many sellers make the mistake of dumping a hatful of strengths into the buyer's lap and are marked down because of their failure to interpret the question accurately. One strength only, please.

The worst you can do with this question is waste it and it is very much wasted if you sell a strength which they don't want to buy, so make it *relevant*. It's most unlikely that anyone will ask the question 'What is your greatest *relevant* strength?' but there is no advantage in selling *irrelevancies*.

In preparing your response to this you may want to ask yourself, 'Based on my understanding of their problem, what would they *want* my greatest strength to be?' If you can identify it and it happens to *be* your greatest strength then this is a happy coincidence. If it is your third-greatest strength there is little merit in selling either of the first two. You may be able to come up with a strength to compensate for a weakness, which you think they might probe later on. For example, if the role will require you to change your established pattern of work, perhaps moving into a different sector, then you might be wise to sell your 'adaptability'. Don't sell something that you can't support as this is not helpful to either party. Ensure that you have *two* examples to back it up. Most sellers would only ask for one but someone of a more probing, mischievous or downright awkward disposition might say 'give me another one' – their rationale being that if that is your greatest strength then you really ought to have more than one example to back it up, and who are we to argue? Examples and anecdotes are essential pieces of ammunition to take along to these meetings; they give credence to what you are saying and are the evidence to support your strengths and attributes. Without them you can be sunk. And don't always wait to be asked for them – poorly prepared buyers (and you will meet a lot of them) will not ask for examples, thus depriving you of an opportunity to convince them.

Consistency is also an important ingredient. A perceptive buyer will expect to see consistency in your responses, often to seemingly quite different questions, throughout a meeting and/or across two or more meetings. You may well be asked for your greatest strength at both the first *and* second meetings – they wouldn't want it to be any different at the second time of asking.

What is your greatest weakness? ✗

This is a monster and is the archetypal 'Tell me why I shouldn't hire you' question. It is worth remembering that if the meeting has until this point progressed in a satisfactory manner then the match is being made, in which case buyers really don't want sellers to shoot themselves in the foot. Unfortunately most sellers do just that by volunteering a weakness that is relevant to the role being discussed. When this happens the buyer's heart sinks because it cannot be ignored and they were so close to believing that they had found the solution to their problem. It is often preceded by the previous question, which gives you time mentally to get it lined up in your sights, but it can come as a completely fast ball. Keep a straight bat and kill it stone dead.

As this is such a dangerous question it is advisable to have four possible lines of defence, any one of which you might call upon, depending on your judgement of the buyer's manner, personality and, not least, sense of humour, or lack of it.

Plan A   Humour has a role to play and can sometimes defuse a tricky situation. It can also be perceived as flippancy or even hysteria, so proceed with caution. The simple riposte 'chocolate' has got many a seller out of this difficulty, providing the accompany body language is non-confrontational. It also helps if the accompanying body is not overly corpulent.

Plan B   As the underlying question can be interpreted as 'do you have a weakness which is relevant to the role?' there is safety to be found in giving a weakness which is irrelevant. If, for example, you are selling skills which are primarily cerebral then admitting to a weakness of a practical nature will not be damaging: *'I've been a driver for many years and I've no idea what goes on under the hood, but it's of no interest to me. If I break down I'd rather make a phone call.'*

Plan C Whether opting for plans A, B, C or D, it is advisable to pause for a few seconds as if pole-axed and stare philosophically out of the window – by any standards it's a tough question and responding too quickly, even though the tape is running, can ruin the dramatic effect. To show the buyer that you are trying to answer the question objectively your preamble can be *'Well that's a difficult question because we don't see ourselves as others see us'* and then go on to sell what to the buyer is a *strength*:
'. . . Sometimes my wife/husband/partner accuses me of not getting the balance right between work and play' and then agree with that accusation just a little *'. . . and I guess I should build more leisure time into my schedule.'* Now disagree with it just a little: *'But I enjoy my work.'* Now take some heat out of it: *'. . . And we don't fall out over it.'* Simply saying 'I'm a workaholic' will not cut it – it's more convincing if you say that others accuse you of it. You can easily find variants of plan C. For example, if 'attention to detail' is clearly a prerequisite for solving their problem then:
'. . . Sometimes I've been accused of paying too much attention to detail, but I've always found that to do this work successfully you have to dot the "i"s and cross the "t"s – I've worked with others who don't do this and they always come unstuck.' Now if you've judged it right the buyer is thinking: 'Yes, I've worked with those guys and I don't want to hire them – I want to hire *you!*'

Plan D Although it's never acceptable to say that you don't have any weaknesses it is entirely legitimate, in the heat of battle, to say *'Right now I can't think of one'* but then answer the question historically: *'. . . but if you had asked me that question only a year ago . . .'* Now give an example of something you were not that good at a year back: '. . . *I would definitely have said that my presentational skills were not good.*' Now tell them what you did about it: '. . . *but it was an essential part of the role and I was very fortunate because my boss was good at giving presentations and he gave me a lot of help. Now I'm good at it too and I really enjoy it. I don't think weaknesses are a problem if we know what they are and do something about it.*' The great advantage with this is that the example you give can be relevant or irrelevant – either way you win. The above example has two other benefits. First, giving presentations or speeches is something that scares the living daylights out of most people, so giving a weakness with a strong empathy value is all to the good. Second, it presents a picture of a good working relationship with the boss – giving credit to and flattering previous bosses will never fail to impress.

Where do you see yourself in five years' time? ✓

It's pretty well understood by most buyers that these days it's difficult for any of us to plan ahead as far as this, which might account for its decline in use. But you may still come across it if the buyer has picked up an old textbook on 'How to Interview' at the last minute. It's a question that hides a number of agendas:

1 How ambitious are you?
2 Do you have any vision?
3 Do you still see yourself with us or do you have other plans?
4 Is your objective compatible with our plans for you (if any)?
5 Even if it is compatible, is it feasible within five years?

If you have a clear vision of what you want to be doing in five years' time it is rarely a good idea to express it, except perhaps in the broadest terms, largely because of the dangers lurking in 4 above. If the buyer cannot satisfy your stated objective you have given them a reason not to hire you. The way forward is to address the underlying agendas, send all the right signals and stay 'on side'. A useful answer might be: '*It's difficult for any of us to plan ahead these days but I try to do so* [2]. *I do like to progress* [1] *and would certainly still see myself with your company* [3]. *At this stage I have an open mind* [this makes 4 and 5 redundant]. *My first priority will be to achieve what you want me to achieve in this role. Having done that, I'm sure we will have enough evidence to suggest where else my skills could be used.'*

What is your greatest achievement? ✓

Select one only. The underlying question is: 'What personal qualities did you need to achieve it?' There is little point in giving an example of something that was easily achievable and don't go too far back in time to find your example. It is unfair but if you do the implication is that you haven't achieved anything since. Achieving something against all the odds will be well received, as it will probably display resourcefulness and tenacity. The more relevant to the buyer's needs the better. The more interesting the story the more time will be spent on this 'why should I hire you?' question.

What was your biggest mistake? ✗

If you are tempted to say 'Coming to this meeting' then you had clearly not done your homework. You haven't come to talk about mistakes but here you are, being invited to do just that. Why? What are the hidden agendas?

1 Are you honest and objective enough to recognise and admit to a mistake? If so, you are human and I might want to hire you.
2 Was it a mistake that might have been avoided?
3 Do you lack sound judgement?
4 What did you learn from it?
5 What would you have done differently?

On the whole we are much more forgiving of mistakes made in the greenness of youth than we are of those made in the more mature years. The remedy then is to go as far back in time for your example as you feel you can reasonably go. It implies (illogically but this time to your advantage) that you haven't made any mistakes since, at least not a mistake that big. You can also interpret the word 'mistake' as liberally as you wish. Trawl the waters of your education and you will almost certainly be able to drag up something that won't frighten them to death: '*Well, hindsight is 20/20 vision but if I had my time over again I would have:*

- *taken a year off before going up to university*
- *stayed on at school longer but I had to get out and earn a living*
- *studied economics instead of maths.*

Alternatively, this could be where humour has a role to play. You might have an amusing story to tell about a big mistake you made in your first job, which at the time may have had major repercussions for your company, but if the work/industry was completely unrelated to that being discussed, and providing it was long ago, then only a curmudgeon would baulk at it.

What major problems did you encounter in your last role? ✗

Unfortunately, for this one you can't employ the tactic of going back in time, but you will get away with giving them just one, even though the question is expressed in the plural. Steer clear of any problems to do with people or personalities. If your biggest problem was your line manager you could inadvertently open a large can of worms.

Hidden agendas:

1 Did you cause the problem?
2 Could it have been avoided?
3 How did you solve it?

It is safer to give an example of a problem which was caused by an external party, e.g. customer, client, contractor, supplier. Apportion blame lightly. It will be a problem that could not have been anticipated or forestalled. If you were instrumental in overcoming it and it required leadership qualities from you then that is all to the good. Take credit where credit is due, particularly with regard to decision-making. Too many sellers use the 'we' word too frequently. If you mean 'I decided' then say so. Yet strike the right balance – be prepared to give credit to others. As we shall see later, humility can have a role to play at these meetings.

Are you having discussions with other organisations? ✗

Or, 'Are other buyers showing an interest in what you have to sell – if not, why am I seeing you?' All the advantages lie in your suggesting 'you bet I am'.

If you can convince the buyer to hire you, then at some point you will be discussing the price. One thing that gives you leverage to negotiate the price is that other buyers are talking to you. Indicating otherwise is displaying vulnerability. This is a typical 'Dead Zone Two' question (see page 70) and can catch you off your guard. There is an inherent balance of power at these meetings which, by its very nature, is weighted on the side of the buyer – they do, after all, 'have the cheese' (see page 37). But in practice it doesn't much matter who *has* the power. If you are coming across as a 'job beggar' they think they have the power. If you are able to come across as a 'problem solver' then they will think you have it. It doesn't really matter who's got it.

There is also great mileage to be had from letting them know that you are further along the track with other buyers, i.e. their *competitors*. Don't be too keen to get this point across. A degree of caution is necessary because they may not have reached that optimum point at which they feel they might want to hire you. But an innocent question like 'How's your job search going?'

(buyers still refer to 'job' instead of 'work) gives you the opportunity to close the net a little: '*Very well, I'm at the final stage with two other companies so things are looking quite good.*' This will almost certainly register – so, not only are other buyers showing an interest in what you have to sell, you may be close to another offer.

Planting this seed can make them react as if they have been plugged into the National Grid. It can now get competitive between buyers and although they might have been dragging their heels until now – boy, can they get their skates on. Whole conversations can be predicted:

> *Are you likely to have a decision to make on the others before we've seen you again?* ✓
>
> *It's possible I might have that dilemma.*
>
> *If that happens don't make a decision until you've spoken to me again.*

This is a very strong 'buy' signal and it's a great way to exit 'Dead Zone Two'. In today's marketplace, indicating that you are not pursuing other avenues is seen as at best poor judgement and at worst negligent. Those entrepreneurs who tell others that their business is going badly may as well call in the receivers. Bad news is infectious and failure becomes a self-fulfilling prophecy.

Which companies are you speaking to? ✗

This is rarely asked as it borders on the impertinent. On most occasions you will be better off selling your integrity by declining to answer the question: '*They haven't advertised and I don't think they would want me to divulge their names.*' There are occasions when it can help your cause to tell them. If you are being seen by another organisation that is recognised as being the market leader or in other ways prestigious, then it can make them sit up and want to steal you away from under their competitor's nose.

How does this role compare with the others? ✗

Damned if you do, damned if you don't. Indicating that this role is not as good as the others is unhelpful to say the least. Conversely, denigrating the others diminishes your leverage. Better to sit on the fence and not allow yourself to be drawn into making a comparison. But give a response that leaves you 'on side': *'At this stage I don't feel I have enough evidence to make a comparison but given our discussion so far this role compares favourably.'*

It is more than likely that you won't have enough evidence, so you should be able to say this with some conviction. There is also something about the word 'favourably' which is neither fish nor fowl. In addition, it begs the supplementary question: *'In what way?'* ✓, which allows you to talk up the positives of the role being discussed without directly comparing it with the others.

Are you ambitious? ✓

A 'closed' question only asked by poor interviewers. You will get a lot of 'closed' questions. They invite the answer 'yes' or 'no' and don't take the conversation very far. If you begin to feel that the meeting is turning into an interrogation it will almost certainly be because a lot of closed questions are being asked and you are failing to flesh them out. The correct question should be: 'How ambitious are you?'

Broadly speaking, we prefer to hire people who are ambitious, but it may be unclear how much scope there is for you to achieve your ambitions within the organisation, so it may be wise to tread carefully. When responding to this question too many people put a limit on to their ambitions and are subsequently left fighting a rearguard action. *'I am ambitious but I don't want to be Managing Director.'* This invites the supplementary: *'Why not?'* ✗, thus neatly turning a 'Why should I hire you?' question into a 'Why shouldn't I hire you?' one. The buyer may not be at all concerned about your not aspiring to be MD but will be intrigued as to *why* you don't. '*Why not*?' is a 'What stops your clock?' question and you should be talking about what makes you tick. 'To what heights do you think you can't aspire and why not?' isn't an avenue worth exploring from the seller's point of view but it can reveal hitherto hidden weaknesses to the buyer.

There is no reason why you should interpret the word 'ambitious' in ladder-climbing terms. Nothing wrong with wanting to climb up the corporate greasy pole but we can be ambitious in other ways: '*I'm very ambitious in the sense that I don't like to feel that I am standing still. I want to learn new things and undergo new experiences. I'm always ambitious to find out more.*'

If you were recruiting someone for this role, what specific qualities would you be seeking? ✓

A peach of a question and one which is really inviting you to give a shopping list of relevant qualities that *by implication* you possess. It is simply a means of getting you to look at their problem objectively. Failing to do justice to this question is a sure indicator of failure to prepare and discourtesy because you clearly haven't bothered to analyse their problem before turning up. What does it take to solve their problem? Does it take any of the following?

common sense	empathy	reliability	fairness
tenacity	understanding	determination	persuasiveness
resourcefulness	accuracy	imagination	authority
initiative	tact	creativity	inspiration
sense of humour	diplomacy	flexibility	style
qualifications	patience	courage	the ability to
skills	confidence	incisiveness	listen and
experience	short learning	decisiveness	communicate
leadership	curve	conviction	
knowledge	adaptability	belief	
contacts	honesty	ambition	

If it doesn't require any of these then it's not a meeting worth turning up for.

Would you say that you had an aggressive management style? ✗

'Yes' or 'no'? It will be understood that you would be most unlikely to admit to an aggressive management style, but before responding in the negative we should identify the possible hidden agendas:

1 The previous incumbent was too aggressive with people – we don't want another one.

2 The previous incumbent wasn't aggressive enough – we don't want another one.

Plump for one or the other and you only have a fifty per cent chance of getting it right – and those odds don't get people hired. There is a possible third hidden agenda:

3 Your potential boss has a tendency towards aggression and this can be a way of teasing out how you react to people with this management style.

If you are going for a management role expect your management style to be dissected and be prepared to discuss it. From the buyer's perspective there are few things more dispiriting than to raise the issue of 'management style', only to be met with a blank look. Good managers should know how they get results through others. It is not so much a question of whether there is a 'right' or 'wrong' style as that you will be expected to be able to hold a meaningful discussion about it: '*I like to feel that I am adaptable enough as a manager to change my style depending on the situation and perhaps the person I am managing. I find that people respond differently. Some only react positively to a more assertive style, whereas others require a more subtle approach. Good managers should know what makes their staff tick and be able to adapt accordingly.'*

This should get the discussion off to a good start, but again, remember the importance of examples to back up what you are selling and volunteer them as an integral part of your response.

SIX

Who's Got the Cheese? – A Cautionary Tale

There are certain subjects upon which people can hold strong views and 'management' is one of them. When contentious issues are raised in these meetings it is essential that you express your views carefully lest positions become entrenched and subsequently polarised. Stories are legion of sellers arguing vigorously with buyers over a certain point of issue, winning the argument and leaving the meeting having won the battle but lost the war. By all means state your case with conviction and passion, but know when to use tact and diplomacy – determination to win an argument can deflect you from your objective, which is, remember, to get the offer.

There is the story of the pompous diner who aggressively demanded that cheese be provided as a supplement to the meal. The head waiter politely informed him that cheese was not usually included with that particular meal. The diner became abusive and decided to pull rank: 'Do you know who I am?'

'No, sir,' replied the head waiter calmly, whereupon the diner proceeded to inform the waiter that he was a high-ranking personage, one of the great and the good, and a veritable mover and shaker in the world of big business – 'So cheese – *Now*!'

The head waiter quietly replied, 'Do you know who *I* am, sir?'

'No,' replied the florid-faced diner. 'Who are you?'

'I'm the man who's got the cheese, sir.'

A sales meeting is a two-way process, so fight your corner firmly and politely, and the buyer will respect you for it. But remember who's got the cheese.

Do you prefer working on your own or in a team? ✗

One of those questions which, by the way it is phrased, forces you to choose between two or more options. Such questions are invariably based on a false premise and it is well to pause and consider if this is so. With this example there is no logical reason why you should have a preference. If you assume that the buyer is seeking a 'team player' you might go for that option, but the way in which you express it may force the buyer to conclude that you are unable or uncomfortable when working in a role with a high degree of autonomy – which might be the very role they had in mind. It may be that the position being discussed *is* very much team based, in which case 'a team' will be spot on. However, they may well be weighing up your potential for taking on another role, with a high degree of autonomy, in a year's time, and if you indicate too strongly that working alone is not your forte they may then deduce that your potential for future development is limited. To state 'I don't have a preference' is all right as far as it goes, but it doesn't go far enough. Giving a straight answer to a straight question can have its virtues but too much of that and you end up with an interrogation on your hands. Better to flesh out that response by going on to give an example of when you have done both and thrived in each situation.

If you could choose any job, what would it be? ✗

Such questions don't really belong within the context of a formal meeting, and are not particularly common, yet it is one which can really throw you at an unguarded moment. This is a 'Dead Zone Two' (page 70) question if ever there was one. The unprepared seller will pluck out of the ether a 'job' which they have always hankered after but for one reason or another didn't acquire. More alarmingly from the buyer's point of view, it will invariably bear no resemblance to the role that the seller has spent the previous two hours enthusing over – no transferable skills. It begs the killer supplementary: '*What stopped you from achieving it?*' ✗. This is a 'What stops your clock?' question. You don't want to be fighting this battle while you are fumbling around for your car keys.

There is no mileage in giving any answer other than 'this job'. If the chemistry is right the buyer will be comfortable with this. If you judge that this just might come across as being too 'flip' then alternatively describe a role/task/business which is in effect the one that you have been discussing but without naming it. Giving any other example is another way of saying 'this role is second best'.

If I had your last boss here now and asked him about you what do you think he would tell me? ✓

Or, 'What did your previous buyer think about the product?' A picture of your previous boss has now been planted in your mind. Is it a pleasant or unpleasant picture to behold? The chances are that your body language will yield a clue. If you look uncomfortable sellers will think they are on to something, and they probably will be. An unruffled, benign countenance will in part be reassuring, but what actually comes out of your mouth must concur with your body language. Throughout the meeting perceptive buyers will be looking for this conjunction between oral and non-oral signals. Such a question is designed to find out if you had a good working relationship with your boss and what kind of a person you are to work with. Interestingly '. . . *what do you think he would tell me?*' impels most respondents to begin by saying, 'I *think* he would tell you that . . .' This is not particularly reassuring. Clearly, the question is hypothetical but the most effective way to deal with it is to give an example of a compliment that *was* paid, perhaps at a formal appraisal. This will allow you to conclude your answer by saying, '. . . and if you had him here today he would repeat that.' Hypothetical questions are invariably best answered by turning them into reality and giving real examples.

Alternatively, if you have established a good rapport with the buyer, why not go straight for the money and respond with a gimlet-eyed '*He would tell you to hire me.*'

What was his/her greatest weakness? ✗

One of the golden rules is that you never criticise your previous boss or company. Yet here you are, being invited to do just that. This is a 'boomerang' question, i.e. one that seemingly leads you off in a safe direction but returns to smack you unexpectedly on the back of the head when you are not looking, a common response which typifies the boomerang effect is 'Well, he wasn't very good at delegating work'. The buyer is now thinking that perhaps the seller is not seen to be a safe pair of hands. The frequency of this answer leads me to believe that it is pure invention – a knee-jerk, on-the-spot response, simply because the seller is bereft of any other ideas. If it isn't then the quality of management expertise is sorely lacking. Should you give an ill-chosen weakness then you are most likely to be asked the supplementary question: '*What did you do to help him/her overcome it?*' ✗. If you did nothing but complain about it then the boomerang effect again comes into play.

The buyer would like to feel that the seller is at least struggling to think of a weakness and it is always helpful to begin the response by taking the heat out of it and saying something flattering about the person: '*His strengths far outweighed his weaknesses, and to think of a weakness I would be really nit-picking. I suppose he didn't really enjoy . . .*' Now, although this is a quite dangerous 'Tell me why I shouldn't hire you' question, with a little thought it can be turned around. This can be achieved by giving an example of a task not enjoyed by your boss, but one at which you excelled *and that is relevant to the buyer's problem.* This allows you to end your response by saying '*. . . But it wasn't a problem; he recognised that as one of my strengths and we complemented each other well in that respect.*'

Has your career developed as you would have liked? ✗

Given that careers are rarely seamless, this is an invitation to sound off about those times that did not go to plan. As there is a tendency to blame others for our misfortunes it is also an invitation to criticise, directly or indirectly, previous bosses – typically those who promised much but failed to deliver. No one wants to hear this. Take stock of your achievements and look at your career as a whole. *Are* you proud of what you have achieved? If you are then say so. If you are not, perhaps you should reconsider your assessment. Are you a worker or a shirker? Occasional brief periods of inactivity are nothing to be ashamed of, particularly in today's marketplace. If you have, for the most part, always been in work then that in itself is something to be proud of. Say so. The word 'proud' is unfashionable these days and not one we are much given to using in reference to ourselves, but try it for size and hopefully it will grow on you. All achievements are relative and Kipling's words remain forever apposite: 'If you can meet with Triumph or Disaster/And treat those two impostors just the same . . .'

All achievements must be measured against the backcloth of one's educational and social starting point. We *expect* graduates to achieve things. It therefore comes as no surprise. Buyers are often more intrigued and impressed by those who have achieved the same things but without the advantage of a solid family background and good schooling: it can demonstrate tenacity, resourcefulness and the ability to work hard and get on with others – all qualities in high demand. But never assume that all buyers have the intelligence and insight to figure this out for themselves – you have to recognise these things in yourself and sell them to the buyer.

Would you be prepared to relocate? ✗

If no previous reference to relocation has been made, this question can come as a real fast ball. The immediate reaction is to start thinking of all the reasons why relocation would be impossible (partner's job, children's education etc.) and then express those fears. At best we try to be positive but put reservations on it: 'It would depend on where you might relocate to.' It doesn't 'depend' on anything. If you want to stay in the game there is only one answer: '*For the right position and the right company relocation wouldn't be a problem.*' But if you know that relocation is impossible surely there would be no point in saying otherwise as you would be wasting everyone's time? Maybe, but why might the question be asked? They might be seeking to establish the depth of your long-term commitment to them and this is one way of doing it. Interpret the question too literally and you could be travelling down the wrong road. Why not ask them straight out if they are planning to relocate? Because right now you don't need to know – you just want them to ask you some more 'Why should I hire you?' questions. If you respond enthusiastically but have real reservations about it, then when you get the offer a simple phone call can check it out. If they say that they are definitely relocating (highly unlikely as it would have been made much clearer at the meeting) then turn it down. Respond negatively and you will have no decision to make. Remember point one of your Five-Point Plan.

Beware the 'nine-day wonder'. At any given time in organisations there is often an issue which, although founded on no more than rumour, becomes a major talking point. It tends to kick around for about nine days before dying a natural death. 'Relocation' is not an uncommon example of this. 'Nine-day wonders' have a habit of invading these meetings and can be presented to you as fact.

Have you ever failed in any job you have tried to do? ✗

Now 'failure' is a topic that you haven't come to discuss but here they are inviting you to do just that. Not a particularly useful question as it merely invites the response: 'No, I don't think so' which doesn't take the conversation very far, and although there is much to be said for brevity with these ✗ questions the accompanying body language might create a problem. Failure can be another relative concept and this allows you to talk in terms of 'degrees of success'. For instance, *'I've never failed to achieve what has been expected of me. Over and above that I set myself higher personal targets and I can't say that I've always met those. For example . . .'* Then go on to give an example of a task you have undertaken, which met a previous buyer's expectations but not your own.

SEVEN A Word about Humility

When you are selling yourself on paper to achieve these meetings humility has little or no role to play. But during the meeting it can play an important part as you may sometimes need to sell it. Most buyers like to feel that they are getting somewhere. They expect to be able to find a few chinks in your armour. If you 'oversell' they might begin to think that you are a candidate for canonisation and must be too good to be true. This is professionally frustrating for them and thus disadvantageous for you. You must be sensitive to this and if you feel you are knocking them for six all the time you ought to take your foot off the gas. If you are waxing too lyrical about your achievements then sell some humility by giving credit to others. Throw them a bone to chew on if you perceive that they are getting hungry.

If one of your team ceased to perform, what would you do about it? ✓

Or, 'Are you the kind of manager we want to hire?' The ability to exercise sound judgement, tact, firm decision-making, common sense, trust and compassion are all qualities that this question allows you to promote. The key to it is the word 'ceased' and it is this that most sellers fail to pick up on. It implies that the individual was previously performing well. Given that people don't stop performing without reason, this should be the main thrust of your answer, i.e. you would presumably take the person to one side, voice your concerns about the drop in performance, allow them to express their views and reach some kind of mutual agreement on what can be done about it. If you can think of an appropriate example of such a situation and explain how you resolved it, so much the better.

How do you motivate people? ✓

Another opportunity to sell your management style. Extolling the virtues of teamwork, the ability to identify correctly the 'drivers' in each individual, intuition, leading by example and sound communication skills can all be brought into play here. Time for another word of caution: *If you haven't got it – don't sell it.* Only sell those attributes you possess – trying to convince the buyer otherwise is not the object of the exercise. Apart from being wrong, you wouldn't be able to back it up. Do your self-analysis, identify the qualities you do possess and devise ways of getting them across, against the backcloth of your understanding of their problem.

Would you accept this position if we offered it to you? ✗

An encouraging question as it can be a strong 'buy' signal. Yet it is potentially dangerous as an ill-judged response can suck you in to a premature discussion on remuneration and, as we shall discover later, nearly all discussions on the price are premature. This question would typically arise towards the end of the process, when the buyer has made a positive decision and is now seeking to gauge your level of interest. For obvious reasons we can rule out 'no' as an appropriate response but don't be steamrollered into saying 'yes' (if the remuneration hasn't been discussed you would find this mildly ridiculous anyway).

It is more than likely that some things have yet to be discussed (not least the price) so you are not in possession of enough facts to make a decision, therefore a qualified 'yes' is appropriate. But be careful how you qualify it. 'Yes, but we haven't discussed everything yet' is too direct and the discussion can get bogged down – you are close to making the sale, don't spoil it. Better to seize the initiative and close '*On the basis of what we've discussed . . .*' Therefore *by implication* there are still things to be ironed out. Now the soft 'yes': '*. . . I'm extremely enthusiastic.*' Now close the sale by asking two questions: '*. . . How soon could you get a written offer to me?*' This implies that you have inferred from their question that they are going to offer it to you – so when is it going to come? It also diplomatically makes the point that you can't give a definitive answer until you have it in writing (most sellers are too crude and confrontational here: 'I can't decide until I have something in writing'). '*. . . And how soon after that would you want my response?*' This is saying two things to the buyer:

1 Don't assume that I'm going to bite your hand off – so think carefully about the price.
2 I may have other offers, so how much time will you give me to pull it all together?

The right chemistry between buyer and seller can allow for a bolder approach:

> '*Would you accept this position if we offered it to you?*'

> '*Are you offering it to me? [smile]*'

'*Yes.*'

'*Excellent – well on the basis of what we've discussed I'm extremely enthusiastic. How soon could you get a written offer to me and how soon after that would you want my response?*'

Of course there is an alternative:

'*Would you accept this position if we offered it to you?*'

'*Are you offering it to me? [remember to smile]*'

'*No.*'

Difficult to gauge where the conversation might go after that, but they are either offering it to you or they are not. If they are, then encourage them to get on with it. If they are not then they really shouldn't ask silly questions.

Why haven't you found a job yet? ✗

This question would only arise if the buyer is aware that you have been in the market for some time and it borders on the impertinent. The not so hidden agenda, 'Why doesn't anyone want to hire you?' invites you to become defensive and sound off about how tough it is out there in the marketplace.

The question assumes that other buyers haven't wanted to hire you. If you have received other offers but turned them down then say so: '*It's important that I make the right decision. I've had offers which were quite tempting but on balance I felt they weren't right for me – and if it's not right for me it's not right for the company.*' This puts you back in the driving seat and politely suggest that the buyer must not assume that you will necessarily jump at any offer *they* might make.

It is often the case that you will get invited to meetings that you are disinclined to attend. Always turn up for them. Why?

1   You need as much practice as you can get. If you are new to the marketplace it will typically take you six meetings to get up to speed. Better to hone your skills and practise your technique at meetings which don't matter.

2   It's not unusual to find yourself discussing a role other than the one you turned up to discuss. It may become apparent to the buyer very quickly that the problem being discussed won't stretch you enough and hold your interest, but if you are displaying enthusiasm for working with them they will be bound to consider you as the solution to other problems they might have – *and which they haven't yet got around to advertising.* If you don't turn up you will never uncover these little gems.

3   You are passing up a networking opportunity. Go along with your own agenda, e.g. to find out more about their competitors, the market or their network contacts and come away with a bucketful of other leads.

4   Get them to offer it to you so that you can turn it down. You can then go to subsequent meetings and deal with this question with honesty and conviction.

How important is money to you? ✗

Sellers have an alarming habit of picking up the salary ball and running with it. Unfortunately this isn't the ball being delivered. To compound the error they invariably go on to eschew the importance of it: 'It's important *but* it's not the be all and end all. Other things are more important at this stage in my career such as doing something that satisfies me . . .' (now they make heroic efforts to regain the high ground and not come across as a

pushover) '. . . *but* I do need to maintain my standard of living.'
This is like Buster Keaton on ice – all over the place. With an
answer like that the nasty supplementary questions are queuing
up: 'What is your present salary?' ✗ 'What salary are you looking
for?' ✗ 'What do you need to maintain your standard of living?'
✗. You would be much better off indicating that money is
important and no 'buts' about it – however, the context in which
you set this is crucial: '*Money is extremely important. You're in
business to make a profit and we should all remember that, and
not just profits but cost effectiveness, budgetary constraints –
value for money is also important. If we stay focused on those
things the company will stay successful and everyone in it will be
happy.*' (NOW HIRE ME!)

Or (just in case you are discussing a problem in the Public Sector):
'*Money is extremely important. In government service we are
spending tax payers' money and are accountable to them. We must
be mindful of this.*'

This allows you to say that money *is* important but because the
vehicle you are using to get the point across is *their* money and
not yours you won't get bogged down in a premature discussion
on the price. It also implies that you won't be a pushover when it
does come to discussing it. If ever a question were designed to
find out which type of seller you are (see page xii) this is it.

In the Five-Point Plan we saw that there is a strong element of
role-playing at these meetings and this is highlighted again here.
With our 'human' hat on our head we can all appreciate that there
are more important things in life and that money certainly isn't
the be all and end all. But when we have our 'buyer's' hat on we
don't want to hear such things.

You do not have all the experience we are seeking ✗

Or, 'Because you don't have this experience I can't hire you, can

I?' Here, an aspect of the role is being highlighted of which you have no previous experience. The buyer needs some strong reassurance from you that this isn't going to be a problem. Our Five-Point Plan tells us that if you get the meeting the buyer must consider that, at the very least, you could possibly be the solution to their problem. Logic tells us then that this 'objection' cannot be insurmountable. Yet you don't surmount it simply by saying, 'I don't think that will be a problem.' This is easier to defend if you have done your homework and asked yourself the 'Why might they not hire me?' question. When buyers put an objection on the table, which they know could easily have been anticipated, their hearts sink when the seller looks mystified – the body language clearly displays lack of preparation and forethought.

With preparation you can really blow them out of the water by giving a hatful of reasons why it won't be a problem:

1   You are confident.
2   You have common sense.
3   You have a short learning curve.
4   You can give an example of a role you took on in the past and succeeded – a precedent has been set.
5   You can make them see it as an advantage.
6   You can explain that you can offer them ninety per cent of the experience they are seeking – if you had a hundred per cent you wouldn't be at the meeting.

Now it's simply a matter of formulating a response, which includes as many of the above as you can support. A useful preamble to your answer is to say: '*I've given this a lot of thought and it isn't going to be a problem for the following reasons . . .*' Now the buyer is already reassured because you have clearly anticipated it. Moreover, you are now going to go on to provide a whole shopping list of reasons – this will have buyers sitting on the edge of their seats: '*. . . First, when I took on my previous role I had no experience of . . . But with a combination of common* *sense, confidence and a short learning curve I came out of it very well – I've done it before so I can do it again. I also see it as an asset. You could offer this to someone who's done it all before but they might get easily bored. I can come at this part of the role with a fresh mind, give it my own imprint and arguably do it better than that person. Finally, I have a good ninety per cent of the experience you need. If I had a hundred per cent we wouldn't be talking. This is an opportunity for me to broaden my experience and by definition that means taking on something new.'*

EIGHT

Don't Shoot the Messenger

When an objection to hiring you is put on the table, never assume that the person raising it is the one who actually sees it as an issue.

To secure the offer you are likely to be attending more than one meeting. The one with the 'cheese' (page 36) may not come into the frame until the final one. At the first meeting your objective is to get to the next. Dangers can arise when buyers disagree on what they are looking for. If the one with the cheese has an objection, which is recognised but not shared by the buyer managing the first meeting, that person is almost certain to raise it as a 'cry for help'. Failure to understand this can result in your fighting a battle over the issue and leaving the first meeting without having given the buyer any ammunition to fire. That first buyer is your ambassador and will be expected to make a case for you in subsequent discussion with the decision maker – a discussion in which you are never a participant.

What can you offer us? ✓

As there is no advantage in offering things they won't want to buy, be specific and talk about *relevant* issues. Avoid repetition – if you haven't done your homework you will not have enough furrows to plough. This question is not easy to deal with if the meeting has arisen from a direct or networking approach because their needs may not be clearly defined and explained. In such situations offer them things which any organisation would want to buy, regardless of the role, and invite them to talk about their problem: '*In general terms I can offer you enthusiasm, one hundred per cent commitment, common sense and plenty of initiative. To be more specific I would need to know more about your needs. How clearly are these defined in your mind?*'

Do you ever have doubts about your ability to do a job? ✗

Logic tells us that an enthusiastic 'oh yes – frequently' would not be reassuring. It thus invites the knee-jerk response 'no, not really', which might suggest that you are too confident by half. Although taking on the right role should not provoke a crisis of confidence it should stretch your abilities to the full. If only to avoid complacency it is quite healthy to feel an element of self-doubt. If you think back over previous tasks you have undertaken there may be one which really did stretch you and which may have caused you some anxiety at the start. If you came out of it well and delivered the goods this could be an excellent example to give: '*Not on a day-to-day basis, but when I take on new tasks I like to feel that they will present me with real challenges. For example . . .*' If you can formulate your response by *ending* with '*. . . but when I take on new tasks I like to feel that they will present me with real challenges*' you stand a high chance of provoking the supplementary question: 'Given your understanding of this role, what particular challenges do you think it will present?'✓

If the interests of your boss and your staff conflicted, with whom would you side? ✗

This is a test of your management and conflict resolution skills, your speed and independence of thought and, not least, your common sense. It is also another of those questions which is forcing you to choose one of two options. It would be a mistake to do so. The sensible route to take would be one which indicated that your actions would depend upon the particular nature of the issue: '*It would depend on the nature of the conflict. If I felt that my boss was right I would see it as my responsibility to communicate that clearly to my staff. Alternatively, if I believed that my staff had a valid grievance I would seek to resolve this sensibly with my boss.*'

You might also point out that you wouldn't see it as 'taking sides': '*Everyone in the organisation should be pulling in the same direction so we are all on the same side.*'

What was your previous salary? ✗

It takes much confidence and preparation to deal with this effectively. But remember, preparation *builds* confidence. The policy of giving a straight answer to a straight question can have much to commend it, but not in this case. In the old days when we were 'applying for jobs' and being hired on a so-called 'permanent' basis this was seen as a legitimate question. Even then a few more enlightened buyers realised how impertinent it was and rightly declined to ask it. It has never been a legitimate question in the wider world of business and, now that we are all 'business people', it has even less credence. If we slightly rephrase the question – 'How much did your previous buyer/customer pay for your talents?' – we can see how impertinent it is.

Does the buyer or seller open at a price? Well, whichever party opens is potentially in the weaker bargaining position. In my experience sellers who give a straight answer – i.e. divulge their previous remuneration – get offered (if they get hired at all) exactly the same. As the seller you may feel that this would be a satisfactory result, and it may but you are likely to discover, some months later, and too late, that your colleagues are being paid appreciably more for undertaking the same work, and in a free market your grounds for complaint are flimsy. Alternatively, if you feel that your previous remuneration was 'high' compared with your perception of what the market will bear and you divulge it, the buyer's enthusiasm for continuing the discussion may diminish because they can't afford you. Try convincing them that you would be content to take a cut in remuneration and they may nod sagely but it is falling on deaf ears. Moreover, carrying the burden of a high previous price tag may impel you to make an impulsive and voluntary concession, which might have proved unnecessary. For these reasons the question is of crucial significance.

Have a defensive strategy in place, which is well considered and rehearsed. Whether you adopt it in practice will depend on both the timing and your judgement on the buyer's attitude, demeanour and, perhaps not least, sense of humour. Giving the straight answer is disadvantageous but it is not failure. Trying to evade the question with uncooperative buyers will inevitably lead to a breakdown in communications and even confrontation, in which case you lose because they have the cheese.

Should the question come in the early stages of the meeting then the real problem is not so much that they have asked it but that they have asked it too soon. Therefore the remedy is to invite them to come back to it later. Now this can be achieved with a simple 'Do you think we could come back to this later?' but the chances are not high with the more assertive buyer. As an alternative try something like: *'I'd rather talk in terms of the package as salaries can be misleading . . .'* This makes a useful distinction because if you *are* going to discuss it now, better to be talking about the big picture. Also – pause for breath here, you're going to need it – *'But can we come back to this later?'* This implies that you will be happy to answer the question later, but don't pause for breath. If you do the assertive buyer will interject – don't provide the opportunity – *'It might be more helpful at this early stage if I find out more about the role and you find out more about me and what I have to offer.'* This tempts the buyer, and certainly the more assertive buyer, to ask the supplementary: *'All right, we can come back to it – what in particular do you have to offer?'* ✓

Some buyers will still dig their heels in by suggesting that they don't want to waste your time by going through the whole process, only to discover late in the day that they can't afford you. This is your opportunity to seize the initiative and invite *them* to open: *'If that should happen I won't feel I've wasted my time . . .'* (or 'It's not my problem, pal') *'. . . but I don't want to waste your time . . .'* (so as it's *your* problem) *'What remuneration do you have in mind?'* (or, 'We can more fairly solve your problem working from your price, not mine'). The buyer now has no other option but to open or back off. In cold print this may appear to be too aggressive for your tastes and during the dialogue you may feel more than a little tense, but with the right body language, including a smile, you can quite easily deflect the question. Maintain your insouciance if the buyer opens at a price and don't stick your nose into the trough. Let your curiosity get the better of you by asking questions about their figures and you will snatch defeat from the jaws of victory – there comes a point when it is too late to say you would rather discuss it later on and you reach that point as soon as you start discussing it. Don't discuss the price until you have made the sale.

If the buyer opens at a price that is higher than your previous remuneration you will be thankful that you didn't open. If, however, they open at a level below your expectations you may be tempted to reach for your hat and coat, and make for the exit. Exercise caution. Unless their figure is so low that you will never be able to negotiate up to your needs then stick with it. The early stages are fertile ground for miscommunication and confusion, and when figures are bandied around they can bear little relation to the figures which appear in the written offer weeks later – for better or worse.

What salary are you seeking? ✗

Oh dear! Now there is nothing impertinent about this question. It is entirely legitimate for the buyer to request some indication regarding the likely cost of your services. Nevertheless it does present the same problem in that you are being asked to open at a price. Given that one of your objectives at the meeting is to find out more about the work needing to be done, and one of their objectives is to assess your ability to do it, there is little point in discussing the price, and how can you cost out if you don't have all the facts? We can, of course, understand the buyer's curiosity and impatience in wanting to know. The best course of action is to treat it in the same way as the previous question: '*I have an open mind. I'd rather talk in terms of the package as salaries can be misleading. But can we come back to this later? It might be more helpful at this early stage if I find out more about the role, and you find out more about me and what I have to offer?*'

If you feel inclined to give a straight answer, think it through carefully. At what level are you going to pitch your price? Give a figure which is too low in their eyes and they may feel that you do not value your own services. Their enthusiasm for taking the meeting further will dim because you are obviously not 'heavyweight' enough for the role. Giving a figure which is just about acceptable to you and more than acceptable to them will typically elicit the response: 'Well that won't be a problem,' leaving you wondering what else you might have achieved if only you had gone in higher.

You ought to have three levels of remuneration in mind:

1   Your 'bottom line'. This is the level of remuneration below which you are not prepared to go. Where you pitch it is up to you. It may be your previous/present level of remuneration. It may represent a level below that, i.e. the bare minimum on which you can survive/maintain your existing standard of living. This can, of course, *be* your existing remuneration. Vulnerable sellers will often open at their bottom line: 'Well, the *least* I can afford to earn is . . .' Impertinent buyers will ask for your bottom line: 'What is the *lowest* salary you would be prepared to work for?'

2   Your 'settlement price'. This is the level of remuneration, above your bottom line, at which you would be happy to reach agreement. You may wish to pitch it at your present level of remuneration but it should, ideally, be above that.

3   Your 'opening price'. The level, above your settlement price, at which you will open if you decide to do so. At what level do you peg this? First, it *must* be above your settlement price, as you should never open at the price at which you would be prepared to settle. The danger is that you could still put an opening price on the table which is below what the buyer is willing and able to pay. On the basis that it is easier to negotiate down than up you may as well go for it and open at a price which will take their breath away. In so doing you can fly a kite and flush the buyer out into revealing their top price, if only to avoid further embarrassment: 'That's a lot higher than we anticipated. I don't think we could agree on that.'

    'Well what figure do you have in mind?'

    'Well, the *most* we could go is . . .'

You can now make conciliatory noises by suggesting that your figure was perhaps a little on the high side and say that you remain interested in continuing the discussion.

The buyer may prefer to choose 'What salary are you looking for?' as his 'Columbo Question' (page 70).

NINE The End Game

Most buyers will allocate some time at the end of the meeting to deal with any questions that you might wish to raise. This 'End Game' is crucial, as exits are just as important as entrances. Most sellers play an inadequate End Game and leave the buyer with a poor impression, often undoing all the good work they have done in the preceding discussion. Imagine that the buyer has specifically allocated fifteen or more minutes to provide this opportunity:

> 'Are there any questions you would like to ask me?' ✓

> 'No, all my questions have been answered during our discussion.'

> 'Right, well I've enjoyed meeting you and thank you for coming – I'll show you the way out.'

The buyer has been left with no option but to terminate the meeting early, the whole thing ends on a low note and the last impression, which is as important as the first impression, is that the seller had no meaningful questions to ask and is thus uninterested in the role. It also sets up a less than scintillating 'Dead Zone Two' (see page 70).

From bitter experience we have come almost to expect sellers to end in this way. Instead of seeing this as an opportunity to carry on selling themselves they see it as one to get their coats on and get out fast.

Having no questions to pose at the end is a sure sign of having arrived at the meeting with too few. Turning up with two or three is not enough because they will be the very ones which are answered during the discussion. Insure against this by preparing a list of perhaps nine or ten questions you might reasonably raise – if some are dealt with during the discussion the remainder will still allow you to play a solid End Game. If sellers ask any questions at all they are invariably the wrong ones. Your questions should be centred on the role itself and the organisation, not on what you can get out of the deal. Your questions can be, and sometimes should be, just as probing as any they might have asked you. Preparing a few tricky questions is a useful confidence booster. If the buyer is giving you a grilling you can feel reassured in the knowledge that you have a few fast balls to deliver at the end.

Don't overplay the End Game and stick to the rules, which are:

1 Don't *interrogate* the buyer. Although the meeting is a two-way process there is an inherent balance of power, which by its very nature is weighted on the side of the buyer (who has the cheese) and which it is not in your interests to upset. 'Interviewing the interviewer' upsets it.

2 Only ask questions which in your judgement the buyer will be qualified to answer. Doing otherwise can embarrass them and drive a wedge between both parties.

3 Don't ask questions the answers to which could reasonably have been found out by you before the meeting, e.g.: 'Does your organisation have an office in Japan?'

4   As we shall see, there are certain questions that are safe to ask at a one-to-one meeting but which might be inadvisable to put to a larger audience – always bear this in mind before the meeting.

5   Although your questions can be just as probing as theirs, and you too can ask supplementary questions, be mindful of your body language (and theirs). The manner in which you pose your questions can be crucial. Be assertive if necessary but not aggressive – you are still being judged.

6   Have your questions written down and, providing you feel comfortable with it, be prepared to read from what is in effect your agenda. You will almost certainly be crossing the questions that have been dealt with off your list. Be *seen* to be doing so. You will be providing them with tangible evidence which shows you are serious about the meeting and have prepared for it.

7   Don't feel it necessary to ask *all* your questions. Only you can judge when it is appropriate to bring the End Game to a close. Be aware of the time factor and their boredom threshold. Putting tops on pens, the tidying up of papers and furtive glances at the clock are all signs that you are in danger of outstaying your welcome.

8   You should also be prepared to test for *consistency* (see page 25). You can ask a question of one buyer at the first meeting and repeat it, perhaps some weeks later, to one of their colleagues at the second meeting – are they consistent in their responses or does one contradict the other? This can uncover confusion about the role and other issues such as policy, culture and company objectives. If they do not appear to be singing from the same hymn sheet it might have a bearing on your decision once you have achieved the offer.

9 Prioritise your questions and separate the relevant and necessary from the irrelevant and unimportant, i.e. distinguish between *need to know* and *nice to know*. For example, you might be burning up with curiosity regarding remuneration and it would be *nice* to know, but as you don't *need* to know, raising it can cause problems.

■TEN Questions for You to Ask

So, what questions might you legitimately ask? You will be able to think of several of your own but you may wish to add some of the following to your armoury:

1   It is of course essential to find out something about the organisation prior to the meeting, if only to answer the question: '*What do you know about us?*' ✓ (page 19). But as the question is not always asked it is frustrating for you to have done the research but not been given an opportunity to sell it. Insure against this by devising a question of your own that makes the point, e.g. '*Your website indicates that . . .*' Now go on to ask a question about what you picked up from their website. Cross this 'homework' question off your list if you have already sold it – no point in wasting valuable time.

2   *Why has this vacancy arisen?* This may have already been explained and if it is a newly created role it almost certainly will have been made clear. But if they are seeking a

replacement for somebody else then this may have implications. Their reply may be the enigmatic: 'The current post holder is leaving the company.' Be prepared to probe and ask a supplementary. Avoid the too direct 'why is he/she leaving?' Be more diplomatic: 'Is he/she leaving for any reasons that I ought to be aware of?' If there has been a problem with the previous incumbent this is inviting them to put it on the table. You have a right and a need to know exactly what happened to any predecessor in the role and the sooner the better. If you don't ask now then certainly do so before accepting any offer – accept nothing until you have discovered this or you could be in for an unpleasant surprise in week one. You have to judge when to stop probing but read the body language – uncomfortable looks between buyers might tell you that you are on to something. They may inform you that the present incumbent is being promoted. Good news, but you may ask the supplementary: 'To what position?' On being told you may ask a further supplementary: 'How long was he/she in the role before being promoted?' This can be a means of testing for consistency. The buyer may have previously done a big selling job on you to encourage you to join their organisation. They may have waxed lyrical about the rapidity of promotion: 'We have a policy of not keeping the same person in the same role for more than two years, after that we are looking to move them up in the organisation.' This can be highly encouraging early on in the meeting but if during the End Game they are having to admit that the present incumbent has been in post for ten years it is not entirely consistent with their previous statement.

3   *Did you try to fill the position internally?* A good organisation should try to promote from within before hiring externally, so did they? A certain response is always worth pursuing: 'There was an internal candidate but we felt that he didn't have enough experience.' So, an internal candidate has been passed over. It might now be wise to ask how that person reacted to it,

because if there is any bridge-building to be done you need to know now, not find out by default in three months' time.

4   *If I were to join your organisation where might you see me in five years' time?* Straight out of the buyer's textbook but good enough for the seller too. Just asking the question indicates that you are thinking of sticking around for at least five years and are looking to progress. Most buyers understand that movement in the marketplace is frequent and unpredictable, and there is tacit agreement between buyers and sellers that tenure may only be short-term, but giving expression to these fundamental truths is still not welcomed in a formal meeting. The expectation remains that sellers should at least send signals of long-term commitment.

5   How do you see your organisation developing over the next couple of years? Providing you judge that the buyer is qualified to venture an opinion, this is a safe and useful question. If nothing else, it indicates a degree of interest in their objectives. If the buyer is patently qualified to answer it by virtue of their position, e.g. CEO, and yet is bereft of ideas, then you just might want to question the wisdom of joining an organisation that doesn't know where it's heading. It's not normally a good idea to ask this question of a panel. One of the dilemmas with panels is that as an outsider you wouldn't know the political backcloth or the personal friendships/enmities. You could be lighting the blue touchpaper and not know it. Alienating a panel member is easily done with an injudicious question in front of his/her peers.

6   *What would you see as my main priority in this role?* During these meetings buyers do not always make a good job of describing the work that needs to be done, and it is not unusual to reach the concluding stages and still feel that you haven't got a precise enough understanding of it. This is a way

of teasing it out without coming across as a complete ignoramus. It can also encourage the buyer to reveal for the first time a fundamental if not serious problem, which they had hitherto not mentioned. In such ways you can discover if you are being invited to drink from a poisoned chalice. This can be a useful question to test for consistency. Ask it of someone else at the next meeting and you may find that they come up with a different answer. Others may be of the opinion that the work needing to be done is unnecessary. Events are changing so quickly in the competitive, particularly high-tech, marketplace that a slow-moving recruitment process can't keep up. From initial advertisement to final appointment can take three months. Events can have changed so much in that time-frame that the role no longer exists.

7   *Can I take a look around before leaving?* For valid reasons the answer may well be 'no'. They haven't built this into the schedule, they have no one available to take you around or they simply hadn't thought of it. No matter – showing an interest in the environment in which you might be working will send positive signals. If the meeting has gone well the question will often elicit a positive response, indicating that you have got through to the next stage: 'Not today, but we will show you around next time.'

This question can be priceless for certain types of organisation. What are they in business to sell? A service or a product? If, for example, you are talking to a manufacturer, and if they make the product on the site of your meeting, *never* leave that meeting without asking if you can see the production process. Many a seller has blown it by showing no interest in the product. Waiting for the invitation to look around is no good at all – buyers will often expect the seller to ask.

Regardless of the type of organisation, never accept an offer without having seen where you will be working. A sub-standard working environment can have a strong influence on your decision and the working environment can be very different from that in which the meetings took place. Don't be seduced by the 'corporate plumage' – it's there for the customers and clients, not you.

8   *I've enjoyed our discussion. I'm very confident that I can take this on and do it very well, but do you have any reservations about my suitability for it?* If you choose to ask this it will be your penultimate question. You may ask it at a first meeting but are more likely to do so at the final meeting when you are closer to making the sale. You should certainly be inclined to ask it at a one-to-one final meeting, which you feel has gone well and at which there has been good rapport with the buyer. You would be foolish to ask it if the meeting has gone belly up – the buyer will have a list as long as your arm. Judge it right and it is a 'no lose' question for you. There is either a reservation or there is not. Find out where the buyer stands on this issue. If there are no reservations you are inviting them to say so. Psychologically this makes it more difficult for them subsequently to send you a rejection letter. You are really saying to the buyer: 'I want to get hired and I've told you why you should do so – do you see any reasons why you shouldn't hire me?' If the buyer responds by saying, in effect, 'No – I don't see any reasons why I shouldn't hire you,' then the outcome has got to be: 'Well, hire me, then.' Now of course the above dialogue isn't actually taking place but that is the undertow. Go for it. Moreover, never be fearful of actually telling the buyer that you *want* the 'job'. Few sellers are confident enough to be this direct but if expressed in the right manner and at the right time it can have a profound psychological effect. If it is a tight decision between yourself and a competitor it is highly likely to be offered to the one who *said* they wanted it. Remember, whether you actually *do* want it or not is neither here nor there – your objective is to get the offer.

But what if the buyer does have a reservation? Well, this

could be your last chance to defend against it so it is only in your interests to encourage them to put it on the table. If you don't they will still have it when you have gone out of the door and then it's too late to do anything about it. We have already seen that these meetings are all about selling yourself to get hired and defending yourself against objections to hiring you. You can only deal with an objection if it is voiced. Uncovering the hidden objections is a key part of your strategy and buyers are most disposed to do this at the end rather than at the beginning of a meeting. At the end a certain rapport should have been built up, which cannot exist at the start. Once a climate of mutual respect has been established the buyer will feel more comfortable in voicing a sensitive issue – and most hidden objections revolve around sensitive issues.

Should you ask this question of a panel? Probably not. A panel have not had the opportunity to confer and you are unlikely to elicit a meaningful response. However, on some occasions you will know, perhaps through a network contact on the inside, that they share a strong reservation. If they haven't raised it you may as well put the question on the table.

The preamble to your question is important. Never ask it simply by saying 'Do you have any reservations about my suitability for it?' as it implies that *you* might have some. Starting your preamble by saying 'I've enjoyed our discussion . . .' encourages the buyer to begin their response in the same vein.

9   *When will I hear from you?* This will always be your final question. Never leave the meeting without having got the buyer to make a firm commitment about what happens next and when. Failure to do so will lead to loss of control and if you need to regain the initiative by following up it is helpful for you to have established when it would be legitimate for you to do so. Subsequently taking the view that 'no news is good news' is mere self-delusion and there is little virtue in not

knowing. If they fail to meet their own deadline it is acceptable for you to chase them up. The outcome of the meeting will always be at the top of your priority list but rarely will it be at the top of theirs.

ELEVEN

Dead Zone Two and the 'Columbo Question'

Once the meeting has been formally concluded you will enter a new phase, of unpredictable length and indeterminate nature, before you leave the premises. This we will call 'Dead Zone Two' and it can kick in sooner than you might think. For example, at the conclusion of a final meeting the buyer (in all probability your potential boss) is waxing lyrical about your joining the organisation and makes what appears to be a spontaneous decision. Reaching for the phone he says, 'Hey, if Joe Soap is free I'll take you up to see him to discuss terms and conditions' (which have not been previously discussed). Having established by phone that, as luck would have it, Joe is indeed free the buyer says 'let's go' and steers you out of the office. You are now in Dead Zone Two, from which you want to emerge in one piece, so tread carefully. This zone is fertile ground for much 'small talk' and you may feel your 'social hat' (page 10) settling comfortably on your head. Typically, it has taken a while to reach Joe's office so you find yourself being ushered into a comfortable chair in some 'mini reception' area 'while I just make sure Joe is still free'. You are now snoozing and basking in your success. Awoken from your reverie you find that the buyer, having turned smartly on his heel, is now looming over you and, feigning forgetfulness, hits you with the 'Columbo question': 'Oh, that reminds me – what salary are you looking for?' Don't bother turning back to page 56 – those delaying tactics and lengthy soundbites don't work in the Dead Zone. A 'social hat' looks up like a startled rabbit and plucks a figure out of the air, whereupon the buyer once again turns smartly on his heel and rushes off to tell Joe the opening price. A 'business hat' will deliver a passable Ronnie Reagan 'beats me' impression and profess to have 'an open mind', thus sending the buyer away empty-handed. The 'Columbo Question' doesn't *have* to be about the price but it invariably is.

An accomplished Dead Zone operator will ask pointed 'small talk' questions, which are really 'Why shouldn't I hire you?' questions with the tie loosened such as 'Are you talking to other organisations?' (page 30) or the more enigmatic: 'If you could choose any job what would it be?' (page 38). But the Dead Zone is also a two-way process so you too can ask useful questions, in a more informal manner, which may not have seemed appropriate during the more formal End Game. For example, 'How many other people are you seeing?' and, 'When are you aiming to fill this position?' The answers to these give an indication as to what you are up against in terms of competition and time, and consequently what leverage you may have to negotiate on the price at a later date.

TWELVE

Who's Got the Ball?

On page 5 we saw how it can be useful to see the communication between buyer and seller in terms of a tennis match. After the meeting has been concluded it is useful to revisit this. You might think that the buyer 'has the ball', i.e. judgements have been made about you and conclusions will have been drawn. All you can now do is sit back and await the result. In reality you have the ball and communication from you at this stage can have immense impact. 'Thank you' letters get people hired and as there is no time to be lost an e-mail may be more appropriate in this situation. First, immediately after the meeting and while it is fresh in your mind, make notes about what took place. You may not be attending a further meeting with them for some weeks and you will need notes to refer back to prior to that next meeting. Make your own assessment. Perhaps there were aspects which, with hindsight, you could have handled better. Perhaps in answer to your 'penultimate question' (page 67) they raised an objection which you had little time to deal with, or you omitted to mention a crucial fact that might have reassured them. It's not too late. The 'thank you' message, apart from being courteous, can get you a second meeting, which you would otherwise not have secured. After the meeting it doesn't usually take buyers long to make a decision, but what are their options?

1   Your overall performance was so poor that they never want to meet you again under any circumstances. Not even a 'thank you' message will reverse that decision.

2   You have already been placed on the short list of say, three people, and will be receiving a communication telling you so. In which case a 'thank you' message will help to reinforce their decision.

3   You performed well, they liked you and might well have decided to see you again. However, the short list of three has already been mentally drawn up and you are not on it. So, with mixed feelings and much regret, they are about to send you a rejection letter. Your communication can stop that letter from arriving and get you to that final meeting. It is unlikely that even those in 2 above will have taken the initiative to communicate. That you have bothered to do so can have a powerful effect.

   'Further to our meeting this morning I would like to confirm my interest in the position. I thoroughly enjoyed our discussion and please pass my thanks on to . . . [if you met someone else]. Thanks also for your hospitality [if they gave you any] and for taking the time to show me around [if they did so].

   Incidentally, you may recall that we briefly touched upon my relative inexperience of --, I omitted to mention that . . . [briefly – don't make a big deal of it]. This additional information may be helpful to you in reaching your decision.'

   If you feel that there are no objections to be overcome then don't invent one. The importance here is that you are bothering to say 'thank you for your time' and confirming your interest in the position.

THIRTEEN Extending the Olive Branch

You can still get an offer even when you would appear to have lost it. But only if you communicate. The cruellest blow of all is when you have had a number of meetings with the buyer, jumped through all the hoops but fallen at the final hurdle. It is a cast-iron certainty that if you got to the short list you could have solved their problem. A short list will typically comprise three 'winners', i.e. perfectly acceptable sellers. If buyers could hire all three they probably would, but with only one problem to solve, two rejection letters have to be sent, reluctantly. From the buyer's perspective, and from bitter experience, what can go wrong will go wrong. Buyers are often no more experienced in the art of buying than you feel you are at selling. They will tend to assume, for example, that the chosen one will bite their hand off at the merest sniff of an offer and they will be precipitate in sending out the rejection letters. The winner may, many days later, proceed to negotiate on the remuneration and the relationship may founder. The winner may go as far as starting, and even be two or three months into, the role, only to leave at short notice after receiving a better offer. Either party can discover that they have made the wrong decision. In short, there is typically a three-month 'courtship' period between buyer and seller during which a falling out can take place. You can capitalise on this. It is quite difficult for buyers to go back to those sellers whom they have rejected. Make it easier for them to come back to *you*, rather than the other seller, by extending the olive branch and knocking the following ball back over the net:

> I am naturally disappointed to have been unsuccessful on this occasion [you haven't given up – *still* selling tenacity]. However, I would like to thank you for your courtesy in seeing me. I thoroughly enjoyed our discussions and as I retain my strong interest in working with your company please do not hesitate to come back to me [implication – *not* the other guy] should the situation change [if you screw it all up] in the near future [I'm not going to be swanning around in the marketplace for ever].

Because your emotions may be running high after getting their rejection letter the above message is not one that you will much feel like sending and you must resist the natural inclination to inject an element of 'sour grapes' into it, as that questions their judgement. But if you send it, don't be surprised to get a call, maybe some weeks or even months later, asking if you are still available.

Conclusion

There is no lack of guidance on how to be interviewed and no shortage of people all too willing to give you wise counsel on interview technique. Yet this guidance is invariably based on the premise that all interviewers *know* what they are looking for and that they *know* how to find it. In my experience, and that of the many 'sellers' and 'buyers' I have worked with, this is rarely the case. They also approach the subject from the standpoint of interviewee as 'job beggar', which leads to the 'sit up straight, give a firm handshake and maintain eye contact' school of thought, which is both patronising and less than helpful.

There is little point in preparing interviewees for the 'jobs market' *as we would like it to be*, or as it perhaps *was* in the twentieth century. The twenty-first-century marketplace is already an infinitely more fast-moving, vibrant, changing, unpredictable and *competitive* market and one where even the boundaries between who is selling and who is buying are becoming blurred. To survive as individuals we must all have something to sell that others need to buy. We must learn to diversify and build our portfolios. We must accustom ourselves to becoming itinerant workers, but perhaps above all we must discover the art of persuading others to buy what we have to sell. *Winning at Interview* has prepared you for the marketplace as it *is* and as it is likely to be for the foreseeable future.

Also by Alan Jones

HOW TO WRITE A WINNING CV

Alan Jones

How to Write a Winning CV is a blueprint for the perfect CV: one that not only presents you at your very best but avoids the common (and not so common) pitfalls that make employers turn applicants down, often without even seeing them.

It examines every section of the CV, providing real-life examples of CVs that worked, as well as ome that didn't. It is an essential source of guidance and advice at every stage of a career.

Also Available

PERFECT ASSERTIVENESS

Jan Ferguson

Perfect Assertiveness helps you to understand more about assertiveness and its importance as a life skill. The book shows you the difference between assertiveness and aggression, and teaches you to understand more about yourself, the possibilities of change and the potential for improvement in personal, social, family and workplace relationships.

£6.99   0 09 940617 9

PERFECT TIME MANAGEMENT

Edward Johns

Managing your time effectively means adding value to everything you do. This book will help you to master the techniques and skills essential to grasping control of your time and your life.

If you can cut down the time you spend meeting people, talking on the phone, writing and reading business papers and answering subordinates' questions, you can use the time saved for creative work and the really important elements of your job. Learn how to deal with interruptions, manage the cost and cut down on meetings time – above all, how to minimize paperwork. You'll be amazed how following a few simple guidelines will improve the quality of both your working life and your leisure time.

£6.99   0 09 941004 4

PERFECT NEGOTIATION

Gavin Kennedy

The ability to negotiate effectively is a vital skill required in business and everyday situations.

Whether you are negotiating over a business deal, a pay rise, a difference of opinion between managers and staff, or the price of a new house or car, this invaluable book, written by one of Europe's leading experts in negotiation, will help you to get a better deal every time, and avoid costly mistakes.

£6.99   0 09 941016 8